Uh Oh Time

ANHINGA PRESS

Uh Oh Time

Kenneth Hart

2007 ANHINGA PRIZE FOR POETRY
Selected by Mark Jarman

ANHINGA PRESS
TALLAHASSEE, FLORIDA 2008

Cover art: George Pali, *Flying on a Big Red Bird*, oil and collage
        on canvas, 22" x 26", 2007 — www.georgepali.com
Cover design, book design, and production: C. L. Knight
Typesetting: Jill Ihasz
Type Styles: titles set in Benguiat and text set in Adobe Jensen Pro

Library of Congress Cataloging-in-Publication Data
Uh Oh Time by Kenneth Hart – First Edition
ISBN – 978-1-934695-05-0
Library of Congress Cataloging Card Number – 2008931766

This publication is sponsored in part by a grant
from the Florida Department of State,
Division of Cultural Affairs, and the Florida Arts Council.

Anhinga Press Inc. is a nonprofit corporation dedicated wholly to the
publication and appreciation of fine poetry and other literary genres.

For personal orders, catalogs
and information write to:
Anhinga Press
P.O. Box 10595
Tallahassee, Florida 32302
Web site: www.anhinga.org
E-mail: info@anhinga.org

Published in the United States
by Anhinga Press
Tallahassee, Florida
First Edition, 2008

Contents

III

IV

Acknowledgments

I would like to thank the editors and staff of the following journals, where these poems first appeared, sometimes in a slightly different form:

Arts & Letters: "The Hinge," "The Kiss"

Barrow Street: "Ashes"

Bellingham Review: "In a Place Such as This"

Mississippi Review: "Poem"

New Ohio Review: "Uh Oh Time," "Having Not Heard Back from You"

North American Review: "Tick"

Paterson Literary Review: "Nat & Forrest"

Poet Lore: "Damaged Goods," "Rush Hour in America," "Warped Granulated Face in the Bottom of a Beer Mug," "Mayfly," "At Reiki," "The Russian Women," "Fool for the City," and "This Religion"

7 Carmine: "The Big House," and "Whittier"

"In a Place Such as This" placed third in 49th Parallel Poetry Contest. "Poem" was a finalist for the *Mississippi Review* Prize. "Tick" was a finalist for the *NAR*'s Hearst Prize. "Uh Oh Time," and "Having Not Heard Back from You" received the *NOR* Editor's Prize. "Nat & Forrest" was co-winner of the Allen Ginsberg Award. "Tick" was also published in a limited edition broadside by the Center for Book Arts, New York City.

I am grateful to the Virginia Center for the Creative Arts, whose residencies gave me time to write in a very special setting, and to the Geraldine R. Dodge Foundation for providing grants.

Special thanks to the community of writers in the Warren Wilson M.F.A Program, whose friendship and dedication continue to inspire me, and keep me working hard. Several friends were helpful in reading earlier versions of this manuscript: Cat Doty, Peg Peoples, Suzanne Parker, and the extraordinary Eleanor Wilner. I would also like to thank Elaine Sexton, whose salons at *7 Carmine* helped foster rapport among artists and writers. And all the others, too many to name, who provided feedback on individual poems: thank you.

Many, many thanks to Lynne Knight, Rick Campbell, and the staff at Anhinga Press, for their wise editing and hard work. I am greatly indebted to and honored by Mark Jarman, for selecting this manuscript.

Most importantly, I would like to thank Tony Hoagland for his persistent support, his abiding camaraderie, and the incomparable care and attention he gave to these pages — true friend of poetry, and a true friend.

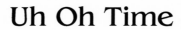

Uh Oh Time

I

The Hinge

The personable, plucky, pale-skinned, slightly chunky teenage daughter
of the Chinese couple who run the White Dragon Restaurant
      in Whitehorse
wears a punk rock t-shirt, black nail polish and a studded belt,
and translates my order
from smooth Canadian-English to the kitchen, in Mandarin.

In white, flat-topped paper hats, the old guys back there —
      probably her uncles —
start talking a loud, jagged, pot-lid banging, plate-clatter kind of talk,
and heat up the wok and toss in my vegetables
with a grand hissing sound.

Her mother, wrinkled sparrow of a woman
with shiny skin,
sits behind the cash register
and rings up the ticket — takes one of the pencils
sticking out of a half-pint soup container
full of uncooked rice,
and writes something down, says words to her husband
that sound like tissue-paper uncrinkling from a box packed
      with delicate glass;
he looks up from the Beijing newspaper in his lap, and nods once.

Call it the hinge of the daughter, growing up in two languages,
who turns on a well-oiled swivel
between an ancestral sea-journey

and Friday night smoking cigarettes outside the Esso mini-mart
with friends who think
the skinny guitarist on the new *Fetid Rat* CD is cute.

When she brings the tea to my table,
I see pagodas and rickshaws etched on the side of the pot
as she pours the past into the present, then tells me,
laying down the check,
she's cool with either currency.

Tick

Little Hindenburg
holding on at the teeth,
its purplish gray body ballooned
to pea-size with dog's blood.
Wobbly, wartish, flopping, tied
to the skin under black fur,
set to pop if squeezed or yanked wrong:
you part the hair, must pinch the flesh,
lightly, raise it like a rug's wrinkle,
then *pluck* with the other finger and thumb.
Slow, beery, drunk on pumped syrup
from the heart of an animal
who seems all heart, now it can rest in your palm —
don't be afraid; it slowly kicks
its tiny feet as a fat infant
stoned on mother's milk. It rolls
on the deeply creased tide of your life line
which a shawled reader once told you was long,
and next to that, the heart line, which,
shaking her head curiously in the candle glow, she said,
though also deep, leads away from your head.
Let the little blimp rest there
in the palm's pink cradle a moment longer
before you flush it — its elastic skin
the color of an ostrich neck; let it not be
anger's target, fear's symbol — woozy
on the blood that loves you.

This Religion

I don't know if I envy or hate those people
who accept loss and death with the balance and calm
of a stick of burning incense wafting up the Buddha's nostrils,
with steady breathing, and a vision of Universal Beauty.
I used to be a New Age person myself, though I never
liked the term. I mean, the only thing "new" about Zen
is that it landed in California, where it became more flexible
than a yogi's spine. But for the past five days
I've been crying, enraged, depressed, to the point of sickness.

And nothing helps. All those books with rainbow jackets
on my shelf, all those tapes with "Truth" and "Love" in their titles —

I'm going to stuff them into a 55-gallon drum
and have the biggest barrel fire this place has ever seen.
So big the sparks will fly up through the trees, and people
across town will see the smoke and smell the burning plastic
and think it just another chemical fire here in New Jersey.
I'll want to crawl into that fire myself, but instead
I'm going to stand in front of it and drink beer, smashing
each green bottle as it goes down, and when all the beer is gone,
I'll grab the big clear bottle of the harder stuff off the cabinet shelf
and spit into the flames saying your name over and over,
till I have no soul left to save. That's what I'm going to do.
That's got to be older than religion itself.

Rush Hour in America

There's a man on the radio right now
with a very big mouth
he says he's smarter than me
even with his brain tied behind his back
he punctuates every yellow light I glide through
rapping on his desk
and I don't know what he would say
about my two unpaid parking tickets
he has some things to tell me
very important things
using his mouth
that is connected to his brain
that I don't think is probably tied
right now behind his back
maybe he hires someone to thump his desk
or owns a thumping machine
some of the big tinted-window mule vehicles pass me
they encase four adults in business wear
chatting drinking coffee
maybe eating a cruller
I'm on my way to work
I'd like a cruller too
I'm the lone American male
I'm uneasy sharing this time with myself
refuse to carpool with the people at work
those vipers
and the man on the radio
is getting angry just now
he's angry at the autumn trees
and the schoolchildren walking beneath them
and the crossing guards guiding the children from corner to corner
and the taxpaying parents of the children
and the teachers too

yes the xeroxing teachers
and the school board I think
I may have missed something back there
maybe he said he likes one of them
I was watching the fall leaves
their gradual striptease of color
I was watching a mutt cross the lanes of traffic
does the dog understand
you're supposed to look both ways
and then look both ways again
now the man is talking about something else
baseball or railroad trains I think
I don't know if he rooms with a dog
if he ever gets angry at his dog
maybe for crossing the street
he could give his dog a can of milk each evening if he wanted to
when the sunset fades like a hard pear
I think he would get angry at me

Warped, Granulated Face Reflected
in the Bottom of a Beer Mug

The small squash of what would be her right breast
grazes Jim's elbow in the crowded bar
like an over-ripe fruit snug in a soft sepia sweater
& he says "Sorry," or rather his open mouth does
for at that moment which doesn't last long enough —
as when a hawk circles between the treetops & the sun,
causing a sudden shift in the shadow-patterns across the grass —

his whole deal — head-to-heart, toe-to-top, soup-to-nuts — is abloom,
'cause he's been staring across the plasma of smoke
at her all night, & she, in her cups, bobbed & tossed
in this sea, trills to her girlfriend in the perky yellow tank-top
about what a desert this place is — *a cultural fucking desert!* —
but he, across the nodding & turning & thrown back
in laughter heads, only sees her opening & closing red red lips.

Ashes

So it turns out grandma wasn't really grandma
but an oak log, or some pine chips,

now that they found out the crematorium wasn't burning
the bodies it received, but piling them up, in white bags,

which reporters say you could see from an airplane, there were so many.
And now Grandma, Dad, little Christina whom Hodgkin's took:

we paid pilots to fly us over the ocean, we recited death poems
and psalms, we cried and spoke to the golden urns on our bureaus —

for sawdust. And all the while, you were feeling the weight of the others
pressing down on you in the pile. Not even the maggots
        could get in to greet you.

There's an ancient story of a woman so loved by a god,
he chased her through the forest until she turned into a tree.

Now that was an afterlife.

Poem

Coming in out of the bright summer sun
he pauses at the top of the staircase
carpeted with a worn green shag,
and he can't see a thing. He almost waits
for his eyes to adjust when his legs
take the first steps by themselves,
since the body has the ability
to negotiate such chances from memory. Perhaps
it is the mild impatience he feels about the words
still ringing in his head, as he makes his way downstairs
to the notebook left next to the bed, so he can return with it
to the chair outside on the porch
where the book he was reading lies flung open face down
like a Chinese rooftop.
On his climb back up the stairs he believes
he can smell the faint orgasmic sweat and private ethos
he and his lover made when, the night before,
she ambushed him on the landing in front of the hall mirror.
She thought, later, sitting down to ice cream and a movie,
that she would think of them in the morning
when she looks at her reflection
and touches her hair, and glares her teeth
to wipe a fleck of lipstick
before going out the door to work.
He thinks of her back, how he'd looked down on it
when she knelt in front of him on the third step
as he kicked and bucked inside of her
in what seemed an animal playing-out of their emotion.
Staring at her shoulder muscles and the faint row
of ribs below them, he wanted her
to arch more, not to curl her torso, because that's how
he'd seen the women do it in the sex videos
they sometimes watched together on rainy, half-bored nights,

and since this episode of their lovemaking
had something to do with novelty and spectacle,
he thought he could want that without feeling callous.
Now the children at the elementary school across the street
come into the playground, making such noises
as he carries his notebook to the porch:
sound of balls smacking in uneven rhythms; the cries
of girls and boys nearly indistinguishable at that age —
so many enormous dramas taking place —
a teacher's voice cutting through
in the tenor of forced hysteria. He writes
the sentence into his journal, first draws a horizontal line
beneath whatever scrap of idea he'd written above it weeks before,
feeling at once the author's words have lost something
of the glimmer they exuded when he read them minutes ago —
what we are left with after we have
brayed and whispered and sung our way into the world,
to which we attach the sticky film of our desires
with a particular human longing that catches us,
as we move across the changing, charged
and irrepressible surfaces of the earth.

Whittier

I bring my coffee to the water's bitter edge
where only squabbling gulls

and drunk long-liners seem at home — and the man
backing up his forklift, arms tattooed like Sunday comics,

unloading crates of halibut.

The mountains shove their chests into the sky,
a fogbank hangs across the harbor like a frayed rope.

Seal heads, black as licorice, bob and vanish,
a bed of yellow seaweed steams in the sun.

But the fishing vessels that scuttle toward the Sound
against a slight breeze — catspaws on the surface —

the marina pilings coated with creosote
making rainbows in the once-clean water,

the float planes taxiing from the dock like horseflies

line the shallow pockets of this town
and rip the prayer from the morning.

Two men in jumpsuits pump waste from a Port-a-John
then pump back in some chemical blue.

They laugh and make shit jokes. It's a job, I suppose,
and while I bet they've got families at home to feed,

repairs to make on their cabins, I don't think I'll praise today
their mildly heroic work ethic

when the gulls have been up since dawn
cracking shells on the rocks. It's just a job.

The breeze shifts, the smell of rot
is replaced by something

made obvious
by what it tries to conceal.

At Reiki

She put her hands where
for months I'd only put my own,
and a few places
I couldn't reach, telling me
when to breath, when to relax.
I lay flat on my back
on the padded table, could smell
the oils she wore
when she leaned in close.
Outside, pine boughs were pawing
at the light gusts of wind,
birds chirped, a car went by.
The music she put on
sounded like the ocean.
For an hour
I let myself drift, eyes closed,
wondering what I was supposed to feel
besides the warmth of a woman's hands
and a slight rise in my jeans.
I fell toward sleep,
flashes of dream coming at me
like fish in dark water,
then returned, feeling again
the warmth of her hands.
Was this it?
When she moved between my chest
and my stomach, I heard,
for the first time, little sounds
she made — gulps
of air, followed by louder
forces of breath
pushed from her lips — the sound
you might imagine

goldfish make, puckering their lips.
I didn't open my eyes.
Thirty minutes later we were done,
and I'd felt nothing more
than rested, curious
where the magic was, the healing
in all of this.
Couldn't I just as simply
relaxed with a nap?
My eyes open, she told me
I'd *released* — that was her word —
at each part of my body, told me
the sound I heard her make
was crying: *When I worked here,*
placing her hands again
on my chest, *so much sadness came out of you*
I couldn't stop from sobbing.
Then she left me, left the room
to *clear*, she said, what she'd
taken in of mine.
The music stopped,
I lay alone, and felt nothing
in particular. All my life
I've made women cry,
and thought it came from
someplace other than my heart.

Nat & Forrest

Fourteen, most things still out of reach,
I worked all summer hauling
buckets of tar up ladders, shouldered
bundles of shingles in brown paper wrappers,
apron after apron of one-inch nails.
By dusk each day, filled with heroes and cokes,
worn muscles pulled me down while the dark
blew through the humid van with the rattle of nail-cans
and toolboxes, squeak of old shocks, shifting
2x4s and propane bottles clanging, as I sat
on an overturned cement pail between Forrest and Nat.

A plate covered with foil waited at home,
whatever mom made that night; I'd reheat it
in our new microwave, eat alone in the bright
kitchen while she watched t.v. in the den.
Maybe I would read one of my new fishing magazines.
Another covered plate sat on the stove.
By the time dad got home to eat, I'd be
slouched before the tube, feet up, mumbling
one-word answers to his queries about the job.

Next morning, up at six, a honk at seven,
Nat greeted me with more cheer than Forrest
(whose skin paled a dusty black when hung over)
joking, jabbering the whole drive to the job —
after getting out & letting me clamber over
the seat to my pail, with my paper lunch sack.
Once there I'd untie the ladders and unload
while they hooked on tool belts, sipped coffee
from Styrofoam cups, lit cigarettes,
surveyed the worn shingles & blistered tar.
Up on the roof, everything ready, we'd sit on the peak,

watch the morning gather its blue-orange blaze
above whatever town we were in that day.
Nat would pull the rolling papers from his shirt pocket,
fill one with a dirty green weed that looked like oregano.
They'd light it, & I'd wait, shy in that smoky silence,
proud to figure in among that hazy ritual.

By summer's end, we'd fixed maybe fifty roofs.
I entered my freshman year, saved for a car.
At the first snows, Nat went to his wife in Norfolk,
and Forrest's next ten years with the company
did not ripen into dignity, though I learned
that power might be possessed by a man
of few words, if those words were kind
and his arms you worked alongside were strong.
I raise my hand to them now,
no longer blistered, those heroes of my boyhood
who brought me through from dawn's blaze
to evening's pale finish, in the summer
of my fourteenth year, when I had no language
for my rage, when I couldn't speak to my father,
when my suburban troubles knew nothing
of two black men living in Newark, N.J.,
city of my birth, from which we exiled ourselves
before the riots, now crumbling into history —
in the summer of my fourteenth year, when two men
cooled my fears with my first beer,
and whose only truths I shared
were those about our common enemy,
the man, our boss, my father.

Crosses on Yellow

My name is Crosses-on-yellow.
My friends admonish me from the corner
of responsibility, prisoners of love.

The streetlight looks like dawn,
like danger. I speed up
when told to slow down.

Wolfish, headstrong, scarred
by work and love,
I navigate by the lit fuses

of sorrow and desire.
I carry the blue sun inside my chest.
The asphalt sea

builds waves of traffic;
I rush to the new shore,
my loved ones calling from the curb.

II

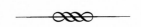

Keep America Beautiful

Somebody hung out his red, white and blue
laundry on the highway overpass outside Providence,

a short distance from the prison crew picking up
our Cheetos bags and burger wrappers

and monster drink cups. We're stalled in traffic;
bumper stickers announce the price of freedom,

claim liberty is our right.
The guard in mirror sunglasses leans against

the correctional facility van, props a shotgun on his knee
like he's auditioning for a movie. He's protecting

our freedom to litter from the inmates' desire
to be free to litter. We inch along;

past the Budweiser billboards and the ad haiku,
brakes wheeze — some like an espresso machine,

some like an aging soprano with emphysema.
It looks like this is going to take awhile, here

beneath the soiled laundry of the republic
which clings to a chain link fence.

Maybe the seagull floating above us
sees a few things that we can't.

He's probably scavenging for something
we've left behind.

Route One

Facing Route 1, east of the city,
a house-sized ugly purple newborn with crossed eyes
is pasted on the anti-abortion billboard,
where the stench from salt marsh
mixes with smokestacks, forcing me to roll up the car windows.
The sky is a thicket of grays tonight, a horror movie,
the Empire steeple in the pale distance lit up green.
Everywhere I look, stamp of the civilized world, the example of us
overflowing — what some cultural journal each decade
labels "crisis," which we somehow learn to absorb
like salt into bread dough.
And the good folk who put up that billboard, bless them,
would like to see even more of us. Which leads me to
the man, a mile on, who throws popcorn at pigeons
which cluster around him like third-world children,
where cars pause on the entrance ramp
and toss coins onto the sheet he spreads out,
like a volunteer firehouse taking donations on Labor Day.
For twenty-three years I have seen him sit there, not
on a milk crate, since he puts in such long hours, but on a chair
with ripped naugahyde, the foam padding squeezed out of it,
empty tonight like a broken throne below the burned-out street lamp.
At this hour he may be asleep on a soggy mattress
beneath the bridge, or shitting into a garbage can, but what do I know,
he could be out with his girl sipping the pain away
at Burke's, or on one of those busses
that give you twenty dollars in tokens and take you to Atlantic City,
where he'll sit at a roulette table and drink free R&R,

feeling like some sort of king. I haven't given him a face
because I move too fast to see it, and anyway there's no shoulder
for pulling over. For all I know,
he could be reading a torn-out page of Ephesians
to keep his tucked soul alive:
… *With all lowliness and meekness, with longsuffering,*
forbearing one another in love …
In a few hours, I'm driving back with one hand,
eating an egg sandwich from the Tunnel Diner
with the other, doing sixty in a glass and metal box on rubber wheels
that bricks me off from the rubble and the trash,
and enough college in me not to care.
I listen to a call-in show on the radio
about Native American alcoholics and sexually transmitted diseases,
and the clouds have lifted, the moon wobbles.
By dawn I'll be breathing deep, my face crushed
into a buckwheat pillow washed with hypoallergenic detergent,
and he, black, blacker than I can imagine across any gulf,
in clothes that smell like his life,
may just be waking from sleep, trying to remember
where his night left off, trying to focus on the serial number
of this month's refrigerator box in which he's taken residence,
while scrubby birds and church bells remind him of the hard asphalt.
And what if that face on the billboard were his?
Would he choose this life amid the ruins? Prisoner
or prophet of the margins, at the rag-end of some failed experiment,
one of the leftovers: he peers at his regime
of street, and dirty sky, and passing cars.

American Music

In the hip hop section of the uptown music store,
two women have it out: "Yo bitch les take it outside"

"That scar on yo face look like you was in prison, bitch"
"You gotta problem wi me jus cause I'm black"

"Fuck you, I'm fucking black" "No you ain't, you — "
"You tellin me I ain't black? Girl, —"

Most of us stood around making believe
we were looking through the "L" or "T" section of CDs,

when a security guard bigger than both of them
put down his magazine and eased off his stool, sauntered over

as he might walk toward a fallen floor display
or a piece of litter he was required to pick up.

Their voices rose & lobbed over his body, between them
like a water tower, dousing the brush fire

which spread through the dry kindling of blond heads
and locked handbags and our suddenly boring lives.

It was like certain other sporting events,
where white people watch black people knock the stuffing

out of each other, then exit the arena through the litter
of ticket stubs, 20 ounce beer cups, and gratified desire.

An average Saturday in an average December. Dark outside
when the ladies were escorted out, lighter inside

where we remained.

Vajrasattva

There's a Vajrasattva wind blowing in from the East,
and it's swaying the very tips of that tree —
from the frozen, oval, infantile nubs
on their way to becoming spring's mint-green buds,
down through the wiry, thickening branches,

moving deeper into the trunk
so it groans.

I can't see the wind,
so I've got to rely on these frail, brittle limbs,
these malnourished arms
spread out like the beginning of an embrace,
                    — and the chilly blast of air
that makes my eyes water,
then blows them dry.

                    Vajrasattva, Buddha
I let into my heart like a little gift box
last Saturday:
                    We chanted
and meditated, then waited on line
to receive a blessing from your representative

concealed in plain western clothing
and a modern American body,

like we'd received communion from an undercover priest,
like I'd been asked to take Jesus into my heart
          all over again.

Instead of a wafer, instead of the wine,
we got a little touch on top of the head
with a bell that tinkled, and some words in Sanskrit.

Vajrasattva. Vajrasattva.
Buddha of Purification.

I'm watching this tall, slender oak perform against the sky,
the sincerity of its gray, pleated torso:
skeletal, barren,
stripped of its kimono of leaves.

A small brown bird lands in its dark, dendritic branches,
sings a quick song, flies sideways
through the tumbling air.

An old leaf, hanging on to the delusion of summer
rattles frantically, like a prisoner with a metal cup
against his cage.

I know that leaf. That grasping.
Stepping forward with one leg
while the other is chained to a ball:

Saturday felt a little hokey —
all those people making believe
        they were being transformed
right in front of each other
like they were at a faith healing.

        The brochure said
this was supposed to open me
like a sealed envelope —

free me from the crushing paperwork in my heart.
It was supposed to give "sublime blessings."
It was supposed to —

It wasn't supposed to anything:

This is Buddhism, dude — Remember?
        You take what comes your way,

then you drop it, like a burning match.

        So I didn't expect this wind to show up
                    after three days, as if
Vajrasattva was a mushroom, swelling out of the ground,
                    as if
Vajrasattva was Jesus, rising from the dead.

Some days I'm wringing my hands inside my heart.
Some days I'm double-tying the shoelaces inside my heart.
Sometimes when I put my hand there, it sticks like flypaper.

But I never expected I could die there, inside my own chest,
and I never believed Jesus could rise from the dead there,
pushing aside the stone,

or sit himself down on a lotus flower, this time showing up
with a crown of flames and a name
I can hardly pronounce —

but the wind makes so much nothing of my expectations,
and whips the dry branches to kindling.

The World

I love the soggy square of white bread hidden beneath an open-faced
       hot turkey sandwich
and the overstuffed plastic throw-away cup of cranberry sauce they give
       you with the order,
which spreads out on the plate in blobby red chunks, soon to be
       part of me.
And the white ramekin of gravied mashed potatoes and another of
       mixed vegetables
in tri-colored geometric shapes, and the songlike chatter of the waitress
with the old guy at the counter about her night school classes.

And sometimes my love for the diner spreads out beyond its glass doors —
sometimes it oozes over the naugahyde booths and the pink packets
       of Sweet & Low
and the paper place mats ringed with advertisements for a local real
       estate broker named Cindy Hass
and 10% off at the auto parts store and two-for-one specials at Kim's
       Korean Nail Salon —
and my love finds itself in the asphalt lot of diagonally parked SUVs
       with breast cancer license plates
and it moves over the road and hops the curb into the ditches and grasses
       and the Almond Joy wrapper caught in a sticker bush.

I wonder what prevents me from becoming a tuft of milkweed on the
       slightly toxic breeze.
Sometimes my love for this world is so strong, it tips over into fear,
and because I can never hold it tight enough,
I wonder if there is a future I can escape to
where I can check the baggage of this world, step onto the monorail
and travel all night at light speed.

But like a shark's belly filled with rusty incongruities
whose edges catch on the smooth dark walls,

I carry so much of the world inside of me.
Those sixty-five people killed this morning by a bomb are inside me.
And the suicide bomber, he's in there too.
I can't see their faces, it's dark — but they entered my ear canals
like ash floating out of the radio speakers.
So now, there is a funeral inside of me.

Now there are relatives making arrangements, and undertakers and
       embalming fluid
and flowers, and black shawls and people weeping in Arabic.

And inside of me there is a sad ancient city,
with towering minarets that could topple at any moment,
and I have to step off of the bright monorail and go back,
it's not time yet.

Back to the noise and the man leaning on his crutch in the street.
Back to hands deeply lined and clutching the edge of the coffin.
Back over the white enamel cups, and forks with yolk stains
       between the tines,
and the old ladies in support hose coming in from morning mass,
and Rafael the busboy with his one golden tooth,
which glistens a moment in the fluorescent light because he smiles.

Against Abstraction

And now I'd like to discuss
the way you keep a hank of black hair tucked
behind one ear and not the other,
      and how, when you concentrate,
            your face twists into four of the five vowels,

and your eyebrows bespeak the privacy and curve
of a wrought-iron bedroom latch.

And while I'm at it, I'd better get down to the business
of the way the bottoms of your pockets
      protrude beneath your cut-off denim shorts,
and when you step slowly out of them
      like a deer stepping over a high voltage fence,

I'd be unwise not to detail
the fine helixes of hair
huddled around your vagina
      as if they are security guards
protecting something precious.

And, yes, I intend to elaborate
on the fragrant rose-pink balloon knot of your anus.

I'm giving myself permission
to enumerate the manifold richness of your miracle,
and I deem it both expedient and proper

to begin with the unfolded map of your body.
Most expedient and most proper.

Because the memory must be lubricated with oil.
Because the soul's expression
        requires a chalice.
Because, in the land of the dead,
on the hills where those who failed to understand
are sent to theorize,

        they put out your eyes
if you did not use them on earth,

        they remove the tongue
because it shriveled from underachievement,

        they unscrew your hands
which held so little.

Ode to Spring

The birds are taking solos at the same time
Little avant-garde woodwinds
Piping their lungs out on the spring stage
There's one with a kazoo
One with an Irish penny whistle
One hitting the same high note
Over and over on the bassoon
There's two playing against each other
Tapping Belgian stones with a hammer
One letting water out of a sudsy drain
One squeezing air from a beach ball

It's that moment when the orchestra
Sounds like a zoo at feeding time
That time before the conductor
Strides across the apron of the stage
And taps his baton on the music stand

We know the name of this tune
We know the woods are going to be one major orgy
We won't want to miss
They're whooping it up like it's 1967
Whooping it up like there's no tomorrow

And we're still finding our seats
Turning off our pagers
Seeing Who's Who in the programme
We're angling our knees to let others pass
We're excited and a little uneasy
In our formal tails and gowns

They're paying us no mind
They're ready to spend it all in one shot
They're bearing the beautiful consequences
They're sounding out such joy

The Blues

Running through the French Quarter at dawn,
I'm breaking my old reasons for coming here:

drink all night, sleep all day.
I've got to dodge the plastic beer cups

strewn like desire on the empty streets,
save for a lone drunk muttering home

or a bright, angelic waiter in a clean apron
who carries so little of the day. At a corner

I jump the gutter as a heavy man in coveralls
hoses down a sidewalk, and ferns drip

from the gallery above our heads.
I'm sweating now, after a cold start,

and keep to the sun, with one eye on the bent
& broken pavement, feeling

a gorgeous ache begin to ignite
inside my limbs, and fan out. I think

of something spirited and human, how we live in this world.
It's true the angels of the Old Testament wore black

to hide themselves inside the night,
but come morning they stood out, & were arrested.

Leaping a curb, I swerve
around a cluster of men holding cans of Dixie

in paper bags on the liquor store stoop,
neon Lotto sign blinking like luck.

One throws a bloodshot eye in my direction.
Blocks later, beneath the overhanging trees

on Esplanade, that old eye
and around it the grizzled black skin

are all I can see. It stares me down.
It wants me to name my sins.

The Big House

They take my keys, my lighter, my pen —
        anything weapon-like,
and won't let us smoke, but men
        pay fifty cents for a match, a dollar
for a butt with three drags left, and blow smoke
        down the john when guards aren't looking.
They bring us bologna sandwiches
        and Kool-Aid every six hours.

Have you seen how captive animals
        protect their food, then, in a corner,
tear at it in rough bites, eyes darting?

Everyone speaks in lies, or truths
        you can't believe.
One man sings a broken blues; another,
        a foreigner, always talks.
And "David," whose uniformed shirt bears his name,
        worries aloud the loss of his job.

Grief rises from these men like steam.
        It has a smell, you know:
part sadness, part musk. Part hair and
        something acrid yet uncooked,
and comes from a place beneath the flesh.
        Some men wear it for years.

Somebody is always on the payphone, curled
        around the receiver, like a lover.
Someone else on a toilet in the corner,
        nothing to hide his dark flanks,

head swaying between his knees,
        the words, *It's just fucked up*
on his cracked lips.

Hell, I'm scared, being only
        white, my first time.
But nobody blames me for this.

You sleep on the concrete floor here,
        use your shoe as a pillow, your own
bent elbow pulling the night over your eyes.

We wait for our names
        to be called — a day, two days,
and any camaraderie we share
        vanishes when a guard barks
them out from a clipboard.

We let our shoulders drop,
        we who remain —
none of that puffing up
        like little birds
in the trees, in the bushes
        — back where I live,

in that other house, where my love
        cooks something on the stove,
and listens for the phone.

Anchorage

The sky's full of aluminum today,
so many bush planes glinting in the sun,
and down here great swaths of mosquito repellent
drift like perfume on the breeze.
To the north, fires burning; to the west,
beetles the size of rice grains
burrow beneath the bark
of three million spruce trees
and turn a forest silver. So
beauty changes her clothes, the old Eskimo
on Fourth Ave says when he tongues the space
that was once his tooth, and asks
the tourists from Michigan for another quarter.
His words have a fine, minty snap
from last night's Listerine & cokes.
Farther on, the talking bear and talking moose
motion-detect us from their stations
on the sidewalk in front of gift shops,
flap their polyester jaws about Alaskan history
and convince us to browse awhile among the tee-shirts
in the ambient glacial light of paradise
and postcards, with bears and leaping salmon.
Reindeer sausage sold by a street vendor.
Moose-dung earrings, and gag mosquito traps.
And wasn't it worth it, after all:
Seward paying two cents an acre
to the Russians in 1867.
Now a girl with fluorescent yellow hair, another with pink,
bicycle past in shorts and storm-trooper boots,
twin huskies pulling them on leashes.

And on the horizon, clouds lather up over the mountains —
or is that snow already on the peaks?
It's hard to tell the white from the white —
and dark crude rushes from a giant metal spigot,
to warm us, to make us go.

III

Monday Morning

They come in out of the world,
worker-gnomes, matter-of-fact,
drop their packs and talk
business as they take off, and hang up
coats on labeled hooks —
We tied East in hockey on Saturday;
My dog got sick eating a squirrel.
They remind you of factory workers
clocking in for a shift,
stacking lunchboxes on the heater,
and those who brought nothing
sign up for what the cafeteria
offers today, rubbing pink noses
with the palms of their hands
while tugging off caps
to reveal hazy piles of static
like pitchforks of straw.
They are frightening in their self-assurance
before the teacher speaks,
when they stop and look blank,
checking their insides
with their outsides, invisibly
patting themselves to make sure —
then look, open, open-eyed,
toward the biggest person in the room,
hands going up like shot stars.

   for Tessa deGavre

The Pool

Aqua, & gemmed by the sun,
cannon-balling brats in red swim suits,

their bony shoulders, flat chests
& candy-purpled tongues rodeo

in circles around bulging fathers.
Mother's bikini strap-marks across

her unstrapped back, breast-sides
white like bullfrog bellies. She tries

to rest, work her tan,
but the fight over the orange soda

brings her to elbows, to scold,
revealing for the freckled adolescent

pool attendant just now sweeping
the concrete a few feet away

something he'll replay later
in the quiet of his room: the cool burn

on his nose, red half-moons over cheekbones,
stinging skin along shirt sleeves,

the too-tight trunks he loosens in the dark.

Damaged Goods

Holly is trying to date again
while nursing her six-month-old, Sam,
still changing diapers for Alyssa, too,
after eight years of marriage.

She asks me, her friend for years,
"Is it ok for a guy to kiss me on the first night?"

I feel sorry for Holly, sorry
she has to learn the rituals of courtship at this age,
sorry she had to find her ex in bed with a woman,
not exactly sleeping. And now

after the fights, sleepless nights, and the tears,
Holly has to start over, practice something
she thought she'd never need, study an art
she left behind in college — classes and dorms and boys —

the way people there read all those great books
and think they'll never have to read them again.

That's what it's like for Holly, thrown back
to a time before midnight feedings, a few presidents ago,
just when she thinks she is getting good at something:

the one-handed diaper change,
negotiating the maze of toys on the floor.

Now the voice of a friend saying, *yes.*

Girl Waiting for a School Bus

Corn leaves tousled by a breeze
make a scraping sound in winter.
Crows gather in the few trees
and darken the gray sky at dawn.

She's too old for her pink coat
and doesn't stomp with her heel
the crust of ice on the little moat
at the mailbox where the paper lays.

There's a plum inside her knapsack
that mom washed; she hopes its scarred
shiny surface of fogged purple-black
is not squashed and bleeding by noon.

Behind her, up the driveway, mother
feeds formula to the baby. Beyond
her two black shoes, teachers fill the empty halls,
somewhere father straightens his tie.

Foam balls and cakes of ice
swirl in eddies on the river.
They're like the crow dad found with lice
crawling on its smooth black surface.

Everything is memory and hope,
but from the scrape of leaves
she hears the bus' brakes down the slope,
sees the grill's lapel, the driver's face,

hissing open of accordion doors.
She is last on the route, so heads straight
to Caitlin Brown, amid the roar
of screams, like someone lost, then found.

Visitor

Three years married, and already something
is wrong, though I can't tell what.
When he speaks, she sits on the floral sofa,
arms folded, legs crossed, looking down
at the floor, or at her knee, as if she were
sorry, the way a child sits embarrassed
near its parent who just now is extolling
some virtue of the child in the child's presence
but would never do so when guests aren't around,
and simplifies that virtue, exposing its privacy,
making whatever it is sound ridiculous
by publicizing it so. Only he isn't talking about her,
he's just talking, eloquently, unashamed, and it —
though it could be something else a once-a-year
visitor, like myself, wouldn't know —
it's making her react this way, so that I keep glancing
at her, hoping she'll join the conversation, but no,
impossible, so I begin to fidget, and gulp down
the last of my drink, straightening up in my chair
like I'd just realized the time, so that he reads my cues,
and says, so I don't have to, apologetically,
"Well, you probably want to get on the road before dark."

The Future of Memory

there are two alternatives,
both heartless:
memory & forgetfulness.
— Jon Anderson

In the beige high school hallway,
where little happens that is not
fuel-injected with hormones,

a teammate asks you,
outside the wrestling room
with wall-to-wall red mats,

if your new Chinese girlfriend
has a *slanted cunt.*

You have just crawled across
each others' teenage bodies, skin
pressing on hot skin,

someone's heartbeat pounding
into someone else's spine;
a bicep getting acquainted with a groin.

Maybe a half smile creeps
up one side of your mouth.
Maybe you punch him

on the arm as everyone giggles
in their gray sweatpants.
Walking back to the showers,

it sinks in — the body's sweet pull,
how each of its moves
has a name, a strategy.

It's Burt, the heavyweight,
who completes the equation,
It's okay, he's got a bent dick.

There are times when words seem to
hook towards you
from some far corner of the sky,

then attach to your body,
and burrow in
for decades.

How hard you suck
and bite each other's throats
in the D-Wing stairwell —

she, whose name
you will not remember.

The Russian Women

The Russian women I watched last night
on my way home from work, dancers
at a go-go bar on a small highway

where people go to buy garden sculptures
and bathroom accessories, are mostly single mothers,
and, like they told me on twenty-minute breaks,

have been here less than ten years
and live in Brooklyn's ethnic neighborhoods.
I kept my jacket on — I didn't think I'd stay too long

but the truth is I look good in it, soft corduroy
that sets me off from the younger men,
collars up on their polo shirts, a boyish need in me

to be thought attractive even to women whose job it is.
The bartender slid me back a stack of singles
which flew off like calendar pages in old movies

when each woman filed past, squirmed a little, pulled a strap
from her bra or g-string so I could press my hand
against her warm skin, giving back the scent

of jasmine and lilac perfume on my knuckles.
The one I spoke with the most, Olya, or Alyona,
names exotic enough for American men

they didn't have to change them,
sat with me and sipped a glass of Chardonnay I paid for.
She was mock-angry — hands on hips, shoulders squared —

when I forgot her name, a little drama
between us I liked — by no means special, each
teased the men like this as part of her job.

From a small town near the Georgian border, a teenage daughter
starting at a community college I never heard of,
an American boyfriend who doesn't know

what she does three nights a week and doesn't ask;
strong-voiced, slender, barely clothed on the barstool to my left,
she started reading Pasternak as a girl, Akhmatova,

and before long I think to hook her with each name
I hang out like a dollar bill: Mandelstam, Tsvetaeva,
— she wasn't buying it, though: *So you have read all of these writers?*

"Some of them, yes, in translation." A sharp, bitten response,
No, you have not read them. These cannot be translated.
"You've read Pushkin?"

A vehemence now in her passion, angry frown
I first saw as intelligence, then beauty, *Of course.*
Everyone reads Pushkin. He is our father.

I suggested that a man, sitting in a Moscow club,
could not talk this way with an American dancer. *It's true,*
she said, pausing to see who was working the barstools nearby,

you Americans don't read. Why is that? You see her? — gesturing
to the blond cocktail waitress who wore a black lace thing — *She is Russian.*
She is going to law school. I am getting a degree in physical therapy.

She scanned the room. *Now Lidiya — you let her rub her tits on you before —*
she is Ukraine. She will manage a five-star hotel.
All of them have read Pushkin. All of us. I looked around.

Skin and underwear moved from man to man like bees to flower cups.
A woman on stage spiraled the pole and slid her groin
along its brass. I asked why so many Russian dancers.

Look, we have to make a living.
I'm not a whore, you know. You want me to clean fucking toilets?
Rent is not cheap. And do you know what tuition costs, Professor?

A half-smile to soften the edge of her barb. "I wasn't judging.
I just don't see any Mexican women here. Or Indian, for that matter."
Well, she said, as she swallowed the last of her wine, and stood,

then leaned so I could feel her breath on my ear,
Maybe that is because we are the most beautiful.
Squeezing her hand on my thigh, she flounced

to the stage in her thin-strapped, satin slip
which rode up over her bottom as she bent in two,
and hooked her fingers around the spikes of her heels.

His Purchase

Choosing magazines from the rack, in the tilted light,
named for what they reveal: *Uncensored, Barely Legal,*
we know what he'll do with them, the lack of harm,
though some would say, *the harm.*

I think, watching from the angled display of news,
headlines trying to pry open my eyes, that he wears
a blank expression when he reaches the register
to conceal what shame we want from him.

And since he knows something about the world,
he wears it, which comes so natural,
just as, after the tall, moustached cashier
hands him his change, and his blue, translucent bag,

he pauses at the store's exit, slides
free maps of the downtown business community
on both sides of his purchase, inside the bag —
to eliminate not his shame, but ours.

The Dead

Two boys diverged in a stubble field,
one dying from injection, the other
ending his life as a boy for giving it.
One being Doug, panting less, then less,
the other Brian, his face souring like a peach.

Wind in the high field slowing at dusk.
Brian's family soon to plead with a judge,
Do not let a second death occur by sending
him to jail, but that is what he did, the judge,
and Brian learned to lose Doug, then himself.

At first he stood uncomfortable in clothes
the prison tailor made to fit his size,
pants and shirt a brown like all the others.
They weren't men, but seemed like men to him,
the older boys in teens. How long's it take

to lose one's life? It's hard to tell
from what they did to him, but Jacob down
in laundry knew one pillowcase came in torn.
It wouldn't matter what Jacob would or wouldn't do,
for years are what bury things. And Doug was gone.

The world diverged in a stubble field
and Brian never thought to speak to Doug,
though it is often said by priests,
the dead will call to us and call to us
as they sit on the chipped-paint bedstand.

Old People

When I think of old people
concerned about the roofs on their houses,
I wonder why they bother. They're worried

about the lawn & the septic system
& the pool they hardly swim in, too.

One man I know still invests, at 88,
in the market — he who spends half an hour

walking through the rooms in his house
looking for his eyeglasses. To find them

he must remember every place his body paused.

It's outrageous, and a little bit disgusting,
this fierce will to live. Who wants to worry about
         the hedges getting trimmed
when carbuncles grow on your hands like red jewels,

when the cracks in your heels turn yellow, and won't heal, and you
have to wear one of those plastic heart-shaped emergency buttons
with a blinking light on a chain around your neck?

Don't they know it's time to go, to make room
for the new models who will take their place?

But when I sit with Doris, my neighbor,
at her kitchen table, while we look over the contract
that will cost her thousands of dollars,

and I see the scars from the skin grafts on her arms and neck,
and the wooden cane hanging from the back of her chair,
and the pill bottles lined up on her shelf like a little army,

she shrugs off the less expensive job.
She says she wants it done right.

She's got something big going on the stove
that makes the whole house smell. Then she brings me
a cup of tea I didn't ask for,
and settles down with her checkbook.

IV

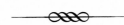

Having Not Heard Back From You,

I suspect you must be dead.

If you are reading this,
then you are not dead —

after I chose the wine,
and teased the waiter for spilling a little on my good shirt;

after the appetizers arrived,
and I told the joke about the priest and the porcupine

which made you spit a fleck of calamari from your beautiful mouth
across the white table cloth;

after I revealed the secret, because your smile gave me permission,
that I love the new movie everyone thinks is bad;

after I lowered my eyes and put down my fork
when you said they couldn't stop the hemorrhage
in your father's brain;

after I paid the bill,
walked you back to your apartment

and didn't try to kiss you,
left you laughing as the doorman greeted you;

and turned to walk alone the midnight streets
with the light of the world sloshing in my chest,

and my skin feeling like the sunrise
on the first day of vacation.

Having not heard back from you,
       I suspect you must be dead.

If you are reading this,
you are dead to me.

Glance

I sometimes make myself available —
flirting would be inappropriate (she's married, or my boss),
and not flirting would go against
every libidinous bone in my pelvis.
"Making myself available:" a little more serious than the usual
banter, looking for any conduit of interests —
"Ulysses" lost you after the first chapter, too?

Every man I know is a kicked flower,
a beheaded chrysanthemum, when it comes to beauty:
will be "good friends" with a woman for years
for the chance she'll turn her gaze to him some day.
And so he trails her unavailability like a stray dog.

In today's twenty-degree wind, my face pinched and raw,
I glanced at someone eating lunch in the window
        of Hale and Hearty Soups.
Wide eyes, heavy-lidded. Flat, staticky hair. A face
that knew it could look out from any magazine cover

but ignored all that, was tired of all that, most stunningly *tired*.
She saw me — and looked past me, tired, bored.
I kept walking, but the look undid me … I felt
revealed, as the lech I sometimes fear myself to be.
A few steps on: *She who was my student once.*
Then: *And I'd "made myself available" to her.*
Then: *I think she knew it.*

Five years ago? … an e-mailed suggestion …
after the semester … lunch? … to discuss … some course?
I think she didn't respond.
Then … I remember this … she had a class

next door to mine, a year later ... we passed in the hall ...
and worse than ignore me, she looked afraid, worse,
as if I ...

But that was all. Sensations. I'm constructing
the pottery shards of something that never held water for her,
and for me, a wish, a slight leaning, now a burn,
toward the empty data that passes through us each day,
each year. Years ago, this was years ago. It's nothing.

But I leaned, didn't I? I left something open, vague,
purposely *vague*, and failing, revealed in my failing —
what seemed reckless, indulgent, unprofessional — recoiled, retreated,
something, shameful to own, to own up to, an old self, me.

Uh Oh Time

It's uh-oh time again when a woman asks me out
        after a year of being on my own
and her number on the bar napkin is the permission slip
        to stop hating myself,

stop walking around all day in sweat pants, stop leaving
        a nest of dental floss stuck to the tiles
where it missed the garbage can.

I've got to start taking better care of myself
        is what her voice on the answering machine suggests,
got to get back on the StairMaster, got to learn new recipes.

It seems the moons of Venus have entered a new phase
        and offered the consideration
that selfhood is no longer to be found in the bathroom mirror.

And because Venus is such a poor dissembler of her gifts,
        because the memo she sent to Club Eros
said simply to put me on the list, that it's my turn
        for the bouncer to nod his head
and unclick the brass clip on the velvet rope,

— Rather than a flower, a bouquet
— Rather than one date, two this Saturday night.

You might think this a pitiful state of affairs to complain about,
        or shake your head in French
that Americans are poor beneficiaries
        of an experience we have no translation for.

But I can hear the soft click and the low *boop*
          and crackle of static
across the TV screen of some immortal

          as she lies on her grape-stuffed belly —
the episodes of my past fuck-ups fresh in her mind —
          and tunes in as I glance at my wristwatch after dinner

and say, "I'll call you,"

then turn my shoes towards the next possibility,
practicing a new name on my lips.

Song of Her Revenge

The girl he made an angel
     by killing her when drunk
waited for her moment & flew in to my arm
     the night I smashed the beer glass
in his face, sprayed a halo
     of shards and suds above the bar.
She knocked him flat before
     he rose like the devil, blood
on his horned head, screaming.
     And bouncers held him back —
but she didn't fly to my legs
     when I thought to run, so I caught
the next patrol car to Precinct One,
     bracelets shiny on my wrists
& blood on my hands.
     "Next time use your fists,"
the big cop said, & slammed the gate.
     Among the crooked men
with whom I shared the jailhouse floor,
     she was nowhere to be seen,
but maybe crouched inside the judge
     who looked at me, hard,
"We'll see you again." Forty-four stitches
     she made him wear like a badge,
choosing when & how & where
     to exact the hurt she must
have thought me ready to inflict.

Fool for the City

You aren't a true New Yorker
if you can't turn a page of the *Times*
in the 18 inches allotted you between subway seats,

so here I am between a Korean businessman
and a fat woman with blue fingernails and an eyebrow ring,
wearing a headset. It is late January,

when humans wrap themselves in wool coats,
so I'm lucky if I've got 14 inches to maneuver.
It's not power I want when I ratchet out my elbows,

expanding like a blowfish — just information —
my mind on pause between "city" (page 1) and "hall" (page 19),
between allegations and acquittal. But the woman to my left,

who can't possibly hear my paper crinkle
with those screaming guitars pouring into her ear canals
like steel barges entering a lock,

elbows me like we're in the WWF semifinals,
though I don't dare look at her.
I only glance at her massive knee.

And this may be another way in which I'm not a good city person,
even though I think she's cracked a rib —
since I don't have the chutzpah to hockey-check her back,

or the heart to swing a door into someone's face,
or push my body into a cab ahead of the man on Seventh Avenue,
walking his twin poodles. Yes, they let them into cabs.

If you put a lot of people into a small place, sure,
friction is bound to occur. That's basic science.

But in the suburbs, we had hedge fences, and wide driveways
to separate houses made of wood, and local stone.

And it's usually a few degrees colder there
in the "outlying areas," as the weather page calls them,
than here, where I'm still trying to unfold.

Looking for Kim's Love

Most nights after we showered
Kim tied dark blue strips of cloth into her wet hair,
went to bed that way and woke up kinky.

In the summer evening she took out her contacts
and wore those cats-eye glasses,
walked around the apartment

looking like some tired Medusa,
little blue rags sprouting from her head.

I always said she should keep them in
because I liked the way she looked
and I secretly maybe fell a little more in love with her.

"You should get a job testing mousetraps with your tongue."

That's the sort of thing she'd say to me,
that made me feel loved and foolish.

Kim's with someone else now,
and there's nothing I can do about that.

You only get one chance in this life
is what my friends tell me.

I don't believe that
but I'm going to start acting like it's true.

Sandy Hook

Rain through the trees
conducting my electric dreams,
and now a mist so thin the air is silver.
Thought I'd have the morning for quiet work,
quiet something, but waiting for the coffee
a long wooden board floated
outside the kitchen window: the roofers were back,
in the light rain, atop their scaffolds, hammering.

My uncle called last night, a slur in his voice;
he'd just got back from surf-fishing Sandy Hook,
emotional about wading through the breakers
at dusk, casting his fly-line, alone, in the dark.
The massive sky surrounded him, the depth before him —
he was swamped by one wave. *You have to count them,*
he said, but shook it off. He was bragging, drunk,
and beautiful.

"The cows are in the surf!" he shouted,
the female striped bass, who love
to chase something called *rain fish*, which look,
he told me, like little eels.
Rain fish: I didn't want him to describe them further.

It was one of those great, dark nights out of legends,
the house rocked by wind, and the tarps
of plastic covering the roof sounded like waves
just before they break. I woke often,
to dreams I knew were not
just mine — someone yelling in a storm, elsewhere flashes of fire.
They'd swooped down with the night
and asked me to watch. The mattress seemed to churn.
By morning, beneath me, something like sand.

I keep thinking of the rain fish; I have them in my eye,
wanting them to be transparent, slightest
of vertebrae, iridescent beneath glassy muscles.
I'd like to think the dead can see rain fish
weaving through the deep green paradise
where they congregate —
now and then a murky, muffled shout
in another language, the metal ringing of a ladder,
and beyond the window, men in bright rain slickers
drifting like fish.

Dog Walk

He pulled me down a footpath in a triangle of woods
a block behind the rental. Seeing no street
he could run to, just a creek, I let him off-leash.
The morning starting up, ducks splashing,
tall grass of midsummer. When I saw
him eat something I ran, slapped him on the nose — no!—
and looked down to see a pile of shit, next to it
a paper bag some crouching soul had used to wipe himself.

Back on the path, clipped again to the red retractable leash,
he led me round the bend over root-buckled blacktop
to sniff beneath the broad leaves of devil's club; the sun
came through in geometric shapes, shafts and circles.
I caught a glint of silver up ahead, transistor radio
propped on a bench, a few more things set out as if to dry
along the path, along the grass that edged the path.
Then a man, seated upright on a blanket on the ground,
legs folded, hands on knees, long matted hair and beard,
shirtless skin darkened by sun and grime;
I thought of paintings I'd seen of the Buddha
in the forest, after his great awakening.

Back next day, he was gone. The bench, the path, all empty,
the only sign of him flattened grass; then there, something else —
silver cigar case behind the wooden bench? Whatever he saved
from the world drew me in. Part hidden by uncut grass,
I kicked and heard a rattle, bent and picked it up:
heavy in my hand, oily, short stubble of spruce needles
stuck to its side, a dial on the bottom for speed settings.

Like a man whose hand touches flame, I jerked it back
and dropped the dirty thing and made toward home,
splaying my fingers, held them away as if burned,

half like a sleepwalker with arm out,
knuckled the doorknob and pushed my elbow,
scrubbed in the bathroom sink under hottest water
my hands could stand, then washed each thing
I touched: soap dispenser, door handle, house keys, dog leash.

This morning, rain. A walk to the park
to throw a ball I keep in my windbreaker pocket.
At the tunnel under the road, there he is,
sleeping, his gear out of the rain.
Next to him, an orange plastic shopping cart
loaded down, a soiled blue baby stroller, packed
like a mule, stuffed plastic bags knotted to each handle.

His head turns to cough in near sleep, as a child's would,
so we backtrack over the road,
kick across the broad soaked lawns
past the jungle gym and the yellow slide, my boots
grazing the rubbery tops of chamomile weeds
which raise a sweet pubescent smell,
while Shadow lunges, glistening, across the wide stretch of grass.

Looking back, he is awake now, cooking something
in a small open pot, a wisp of steam rising,
his outline cast against the light of the tunnel's end —
like a man in a cave, hunched before the day's first flame.

Big Western: The Sequel

It's taken all these years to figure out
that the woman for me is not the one I can't have —

that far off beauty at the prairie's edge
nibbling tufts of vanity, whose charm
and great smile I mistook for possibility;

that Scorpio who lit the bedroom on fire,
then sharpened her spike heel
on the whetstone of my heart.

Taken all these dumb years to understand the part
in the movie where the hero gets what he wants
because he stops, finally, chasing it. And lets

the villain, the suitcase full of money,
the lost ark of his dad's love,
his teenage daughter's impossible friendship,
come to him.

I played the part awfully well.
They were going to give me an Oscar
for my role as the man

who wouldn't let the love of one woman
corral him
into a lawn of trimmed grass.

The men in the dark theater cheered
when I broke loose
to gallop the fenceless pasture of wild clover.

The women rolled their eyes
and got up for popcorn.

I never knew the halter
you carried toward me
would steady the horse I rode

as you patted its neck,
then climbed on and led us
toward those foothills

with their muted beauty
and reassuring inclines.

Tools

I read ten pages this morning and didn't think of you once. They were clever, smart-aleck pages with stupendous imagery and spot-on timing. But each concealed its motive more acutely than the man across the room in a blue button down shirt who has brushed all the hair on the back of his head forward. And so looks ridiculous. It covers his forehead and half of both cheeks. What his friends must think, older men his age. The pages resembled tools and were therefore functional with their moving parts. Some were farming implements and some were jackhammers, waking city dwellers. Some had multiple personalities, like Swiss army knives, and moved with well-oiled precision. The more I stared each one down, the less it revealed. I thought they might crack under pressure, and felt like a therapist, reading a smirk on a client's face, imagining what it might tell me about his mother. Don't get me wrong. So many pages resemble a box of used tissues, it's no surprise the market would correct itself. And the man with the hair of course looks pathetic in his inability to make his mask function properly. So you see, why would I think of you, a thousand miles southeast of this plate of crumb cake, with nothing to hide but the grace I've imagined in your limbs. I can't recall how many years separate this moment from my last true plunge into unedited longing, but it must have been by some mathematical equation where distance compounds the nearness of death. There's a woman on line for coffee wearing a shirt you would look better in. Or out of. It is lime green: not the bitter, exterior skin of the lime, but the flesh, that other color, seen when you slice it open with a knife, bright translucence, sucking the light out of the room.

The Kiss

I don't know if the way   the kiss moved sideways through my body
was a curse, but it spanned a gulf   that hadn't seen water.
When I say there were wings, I mean   a small bird
cut a path through the breath   that was waiting to be crossed —
transom, trajectory.   It was as if water slid
up against an organ I couldn't name.   It was stranger than that.
Because of the velocity of air, you see,   crossing the sill
of her bottom lip,   which was the last thing I saw —
the dark chapped pink,   the light lines, crazed. Then
the instant was over, then the moment   of our eyes, which were tired,
because it was late. When I say   I don't know if it was a curse
— if the kiss was a curse —   I mean it was like a cup
had spilled, because the table was crooked,   and you could see
the stain spread across its white surface   get darker, where it pooled
against the lip at the edge   of the table, a lip
you wouldn't have known was there   had the cup   not spilled.
The cup   was light, disposable   and could not have tipped
but for that startled gust   of wind.

In a Place Such as This

It used to be I'd pull off the main highway
on long trips such as this and unroll my bag
and sleep out under the stars.
The whippoorwills and crickets would speak
to me. The night air invigorating, close.
Tonight I'm satisfied with this motel —
the cheap, synthetic smell of the room,
the hum of the air conditioner.
It is the gritty in me that wants this,
the remote-control light in my fingers,
a pint of something hard on the nightstand.
In the lounge are men in baseball caps,
a barmaid beyond the ache of her years
and a forgotten hairdo. In a place
such as this, all across America,
the single rooms nearly full, I can almost
expect to hear a gunshot on the other side
of the wall. Television offers no solace,
nor the black square of the Gideon's, and I feel nostalgic
toward an evening of 1940-something, that this
scene should be black and white, my hair greased
back, face unshaven, last cigarette.
But this is the new millenium, and I am in
the wayward drift of roadside America,
headlights still burning in my eyes.
If I had any strength, I'd have
gone to the woods. If I had any hope,
I'd call an old lover. But this rotten decadence —
lounging in a cool room in nothing but underwear,
I need a motel tonight to accentuate the vacancy
beside me in the bed, a plasterboard ceiling
amputating the vocal wisdom of the stars.
In a belly sick with fast food and caffeine,

I slop down more loneliness till the burn
gets so hot it becomes numb.
And when sleep comes like a shut door,
I dream I can smell burnt gunpowder
drifting in from the night.

Elegy

Each time I reach back from my chair to pull
the coffee cup from the narrow sill, a dozen juncos outside,
snapping millet seeds in their tough beaks,
and cracked corn, thistle, and black-shelled sunflower seeds,
scatter into the twisted rhododendron branches
in ragged flight.

To them I might be the shadow that moves
behind the straight-edged hill with its glassy woods
they try to fly through, but fly against,
banging their thin skulls, each of us
framed to window-size.
Or I — have they any sense of "you" or "I"? —
the entire house itself.

I'd like to open the window to see how they'll respond
to Bill Evans on the stereo, just before he died in '78,
playing "When I Fall In Love." And halfway into my cup
the birds seem less afraid

that I have baited them for anything more evil
than the peace they lay on my mind.

Each time I reach back,
1978 flutters in through Chris:
red hair, freckles, and though
his nose curved like a beak,
people sometimes confused us.

Once, with Margaret & Geraldine,
four of us followed a brook to a dark tunnel
where we paired off, sat on opposite concrete banks,
& kissed.

Margaret's soft mouth, the cool stone
we leaned against, her naked arms.

Last night from this very spot I saw
a red fox, dog or vixen — I couldn't tell, its fat tail bouncing
above the driveway's long ice.
When I craned
my neck and followed it, never breaking stride it slunk
up the small ravine where the pachysandra stays green

under the moony lamp on the power company's meter pole,
which clicks on at sundown and spills into my bedroom
with enough milk-dim incandescence
to resemble moonlight.

The fox was gone in seconds —
maybe on the way to the night's third gut-pile
left behind by deer hunters, eating just the livers
and the hearts, if the hunters didn't take them home
to fry in butter.

I picture a map on the ceiling of every scavenger's skull
in these woods — 'coon, blue jay, opossum, owl, weasel & crow —
with tiny red blinking lights for each gut-shot buck,
all the road-killed brethren, each full and stinking
trash can behind houses unguarded by dogs.

A year later, Chris's parents moved to Irvington,
he changed schools, and news reached us
through scattered classmates, he'd been raped and shot
in the back of a car outside the Quick Check.

The gun in his mouth, like a kiss.

My friend, Sal, the plumber's son, said,
"I'll tell you what. Some guy stuck his dick
up my ass, I'd *beg* him to blow me away."

The cold inch of open window blowing against it,
there's a sip of undrinkable mud left in my cup.

I wish I could say the juncos have returned for "Blue in Green."

One came back, for a moment, just one,
so in-between dark slate and washed gray
I couldn't tell if it was male or female;

it pecked and hopped a moment, but having none other
to watch as it fed, it hesitated, and jerked its glances
between the food and the sky, food and sky, no one watching

but me, a lunge away — an arm, an evolution, an elegy away —

behind the pane of shiny glass, before it flew.

Mayfly

Still clung a mayfly husk
to the lace outer curtain
of the shower. She must have flown in
from the woods beyond my window
propped open with a black film canister.

I scrape her into my palm,
place her on the white universe
of the tub. Gray, wingless,
she is carried off by a tiny wind
my hand makes as it reaches toward her.

* *

Yesterday I saw you — cream colored, tall wings
and arcing tail, lit upon the outside window pane
above my bed as I half-listened to a woman's voice
on the phone. I studied you while
she raved of her new love

in Tennessee — for years I called when I knew
I'd be passing through, frisking her
for boyfriends, to see whether I should stop.
It was turning evening, cooler, so I pressed
my thumb against the glass to warm you.
You didn't move. Then you rose,

weightless, toward the sound of the stream.

About the Author

Kenneth Hart received an MFA from Warren Wilson College in 1998. He teaches writing at New York University, works in the family roofing business, and gives readings and workshops for the Geraldine R. Dodge Foundation. His book reviews appear regularly in *Journal of New Jersey Poets*. He is the 2007 co-winner of the Allen Ginsberg Award, and the recipient of the 2008 editor's prize for *New Ohio Review*. He lives in Long Valley, NJ, and spends his summers in Alaska.